AF413167

Sky Yah-Yah

Sky Yah-Yah

Poetry About Life

Krystal Alicia Barrett

DEDICATION

This book is dedicated to my daughter.

CONTENTS

"The sky is not a limit."
~*Sky Yah Yah*

SKY YAH

The sky is not a limit
because the galaxy takes you further
but within the galaxy, there's always a sky
as we get deeper it leads to the universe
we guide our mind

MISTLETOE

Is Christmas time
Chris came by another year
Right on time
Under the mistletoe
Sleepy fine
Christmas on set
Keeping that 100% life
Christmas yes

DRESS CODE

I know I may not have the outfits
Or the cars to brighten your fascination
Hope I can gain the attention by my choice of words
And my writing determination

"Hope I can gain the attention by my choice of words."

NEW YEAR

Let's welcome everyone it's a new year
2024 I'm going to get my gear
 I'm walking in my Calvin Klein heels to my submarine
ohh dear
asking if Pluto is our next stop yes we're going there
submarine cruising is how I got here
trying to work these moves
these move shottie hottie
ohh yeah
2024
I'm going to go my hardest rock this beat
while I'm grinding
turn this over into a harvest
can't waste this treat because I'm going to feel heartless
money
money loves me
gotta make moves regard yet
I'm going to track this flow and
turn it into a diamond shining in my sky
2024 timeless triple N on duty because it's priceless
making every turn over surprise guest is 2024 bitch
and 2024 its rich
I'm gonna walk in and keep it crips

CONCEPT

I work to explore it
I didn't want to lose my innocence
Just needed the words
But I didn't want to be left in depression
Wanted the conclusion
So I can teach about the expression
Wanted the heat
So I can work on the cool
The steps were out of order but still organized, not worried about a disaster

WORLD

Journey in a world to find life
Had to learn by the moments
Wondering if it's the right one
It was hard times
When days became gone
Had to engage in a society
Where you have to save a little to get better plans
If you don't put out in that chance
When the time comes again
It will be like art
Creativity to make a start

ILLUSION

I may come as an illusion of Christ
my words bring inspiring to define in ways to create more
definition
to see the mind
no disrespect
retreat to find the miscommunication that weakens the
time
why are you upset if you know it's all lies
not worried it gave me subjects and leads to good topics
so
now i can write my next book
so good look

CENTURIES

In these centuries
We started with leaves as underwear
They couldn't bear the sun,
Hardly flowing water
Coming up time was squared
Now it's changed
The work is now easier over the years
Lands and islands are now gained
We have top people that migrated with fame
We war even with our kind because we are
Troopers in the game

MY ISLAND

My island is the best
I'm not the only island
Yeah, I got that Jamaican money
That different kind of black
We see our faces printed on it
Those other black nations
Got nothing on us
We number one
Not worried about voodoo
Still playing your old cards
Yeah, I'm making moves on you.
Yes, I stay far

Then when you look,
I'm there like a Coast Guard

BIBLES

My Bible don't always talk about God
Sometimes it's the book of the seven continents
Learn about how I got originated
When I'm ready next is
How to be part of the government
To build constructions
Fun time pick up the army codes book
For war and regular days
My chosen Bible is the signs of life and death
When heavens and hells open

ETC.

I wanted to be a forensic scientist
I didn't want to walk in as an investigator
They said I couldn't go to the army because I had
schizophrenia
So I had to come in as the military owner
Wanted to have a house, but owned whole scheme
The contracts holder
Wanted to go grocery shopping from my own farm

CHARACTER

A person with different personalities
is open to their own mind
You say don't change yourself
But you have different classifications
Sometimes I dress for other formations
To show my attitude
So don't second guess when I get your attention
I use my words and you see my perfection

"I use my words and you see my perfection."

YEAH, I'M BLACK

Yeah, I'm Black
If you said you were done building
Because you were slaved, you lost me
you don't want to be a farmer
had some bad memories about cotton
yeah, you lost me
we have to organize together
not because I'm a leader doesn't mean I don't work
The math is in controlling
You have to be that person you can't friend everyone

STATION

Got gas stations I'm the person
Operating many cars
My style is hot got inventory in every class
Whether it's electric or gas
You're moving and getting past
Got me beat beating for this cash
I ain't sleep sleepin', so think fast
Plans to go to work
With little writing on the side

JOURNEY

Putting aside to find my own soul
Finding new lives in the cycle of time zones
In the whisperer, we speak
To keep our mind on set
To project the galaxy
Got to move on types of flex
The president is flowing
In a new beginning
A journey well kept

"A journey well kept."

PULLING UP

I'm police in the morning, military at night
Don't have to worry about cars
Because we undercovers and we ridin'
Helicopters in the air when we just don't care
Hospital building up
My psycho is on maintaining
Turn over a Walmart so I don't have to worry about
housing
Submarine in the deep ocean
When I wanna go fishing
My food is diversified
With different menus because I'm classified
Relaxing in the train when I'm trying to romanticize

RETIREMENT

Saving towards my retirement
These rocks I've been climbing
To live glamorous it's all in timing
To drive spaceships and cruise electric cars
Still rock the cradle
And two step my stilettos hard
Working on my grind
To flow like the wind
Thinking about that next life
Holding on like cat type
Throwing away memories to be the best wife
To put away for that private night
Yeah, retirement

GOONE

What's a goone to a goblin
Yeah
You better watch what you talkin'
Yeah
There's no fool in this game
Gotta be a player, no hate
Working on my experience to collaborate
Turning up, hoping I ain't late
Got lyrical hits lined up to get this weight
Stack it in bricks and keep it coming all the way

JOB

Building multiple court houses,
So they see me in my courtroom
Medication not a problem,
I've got pharmacies lined out for my appearances
Got banks for my different currencies
Don't worry about me, I'm coming with talents
Not on stages, a 9 to 5 balance

KIND OF LOVE

Slow walk after school kind of love
Make it look like we went to school kind of love
Missed prom because we went to different schools kind
of love
Working together to make ends meet kind of love
Tell the same lie to see each other kind of love
I'll be there even when I'm not there kind of love

DON'T WALK

They say buy someone shoes
They walk out of your life
This is why I buy you shoes
Come get me
In my coldest nights
Check on me when I'm not so bright
Always understand
I want you closer not further
And love me like no other

BOYISH

Life had just turned the page
Misled, became unfold
She was a girl who had to play the role
She pretended to be a boy
Things got intense time to time
It was clever and she played her part
Fulfilled the moments and carried us far

"*It was clever and she played her part.*"

DOCTOR

Yeah your doctor doing clockwork
Maintaining my hospital
I'm going to check in sometime, I'm the nurse
Just inspecting to keep it worth
How I thought about being a nurse
Write my song to this beat I'm feeling
Let it have flow.
Yes, I'm willing

EIGHT

Although they've been saying, I've been sexing since eight
Sixteen come find out I was a virgin and say wait
Gimme
Gimme pussy and do
Ball out in this place
Girl, your body good, I can feel you vibrate
I tell him don't take my pussy if he can't stay
Yeah, temptation is a bitch,
So I gotta keep my mind on straight
I refuse to lose this because he wanna play
Hit and run for the next cake

THINGS CHANGE

Set up this was called - my back was against the wall
My own kind threw the ball
She would have had us in fire to lose it all
First, they teach me not to trust them
Now they want to compare battles
With the wrong men
That's bundling to make win

"My back was against the wall."

SOULS IN AND OUT

Death has a sign morning day and night
Whether you go to hell or heaven
The gateways are always opening
Be careful and read the signs
If you migrated to a new destination
Your soul will come as you combine

WHAT HAPPENED

Having changing days
Things haven't been the same
A culprit stumbled on me
Trying to get me in vain
Paving her ways
Trying to get a good name
I can show that bitch fame
Talking about dance moves
Watch me organize this book
I got game

HUNGRY

I didn't just want a plate of food
I wanted the acres
The wild beach with caves
I wanted to live
Where I can project the moon and the sun
In my every location to create fiction
Now when I eat I can do my predictions

NUMBERS

TRN offices posted on my Jamaican side
Register at my Social Security because
Now I'm American pride
Counting up these numbers to provide
Multiply this money
To bring me high

EXPRESSING

The start was so cold, leaving memories
At an age so young I had enemies
As the days began I felt the heat
The music became one
As I rock and lean
Left with an unbelief
How to work these streets
With good plans turning up ain't cheap
Keeping these lyrics going
No, I don't feel weak

NO TOPIC YET

He said she had no teeth
I said "I'm gonna get retainers"
My head game good it make you learn I'm your teacher
Got you in class because we the new generation builders
Working out a New World with filters
Come in with the next step
To be smart about this hustle, and start being inventors

ACCEPT

I accepted my wrongs
Trying to pull through working on my strong
Hard to believe I had searched where I belong
It was like an exercise trying to create my next song
It was like a crazy move, but according to plan
Yeah, I walked with no shoes but you saw me
Dash out my hand
I accepted my wrongs coming back with great plans
Flying in the sky, hope I fly in good hands
Regrouping to a level that's on top with good eyes
Coming for my position,
Give thanks to the Most High
Working on my skills
To shape up these thighs

NO SHOES

Fell at the feet of the wrong doorstep
She underestimated me because
I was homeless
When I go back to work
I'm not at the beginning
Got many projects to keep these words coming
Like new designs all set

WOMAN GOD

A woman I was called
Creation to life I had to resolve
A woman made attire as it evolved
How to create a man design
To help brace up these walls
Woman is also God
And the work is fair
In these patterns of my own kind
I can worship and divine
To uplift the kingdom in a woman that's how far

"Woman is also God."

MOVE

Krystal on one of her many avenues
On my highway to get my revenue
Click clock my back road has good reviews
Changing lights
On every view
A classic ride
That's how we move

WITH IT

These nights get deeper, roads cut steeper
I'm coming for the money like an eight hundred striding
meter
Yea I set the pace, every morning race
Bobbin' to the beat,
Feeling the cool old breeze
You just met another girl who knows how to get on her
feet
Got to accelerate this love I'm feeling now
I'm back to this money and keeping it billions

DEALS

Many, many, many projects
Working out deals
Like my fertile eggs to wealthy trying to have couples
Making ends to do that shuffle
Have it like a list of goals
Top things that make money unfold

GO-GO

I ain't little no more
Let's do the Go-Go now
I could grab on it slow
And do the Go-Go now
I'm at the age
To do the Go-Go now
Break it down close
Do the Go-Go now

PASSIONATE

The love was like a home
We were together, not worrying about the surrounding
Our strength with each other breaks them all
The love was taking its time to fulfill the memories
Passion of a trust
Then in love is where I want to be
Connecting the dots
To grow with every part of me

GPS

Curve my own roads
Put me on the GPS
Let's get low
How wow Pop pop
We go yeah, yeah
Meet me in my secret ocean
That starts to connect the rest
So everywhere I go my road's on the GPS

SIDE

White power I cross my side
Both my tree of half
How to separate my crazy past
Two of the same DNA can put together
Don't have to touch you to complete the matter
For me to teach you things to discover
Your tolerance is under the level
But it's okay in the data
Keep in maintaining things I rather
To go through this chapter and do it with pleasure

VISION

Wanted to be someone
Had to show more than just a sex appeal
Not because you don't have strength to work like a man
But you can be just as educated
We have the same care
He holds the sperm
Then you gave it to me

SEXY GIRL NOW

Wanted to touch me when I was a little girl
Now I'm grown
You can't stand that I do that thing
Call sexy girl
Shy ain't shy in the eye of fear
So to let you know, I'm grown in here

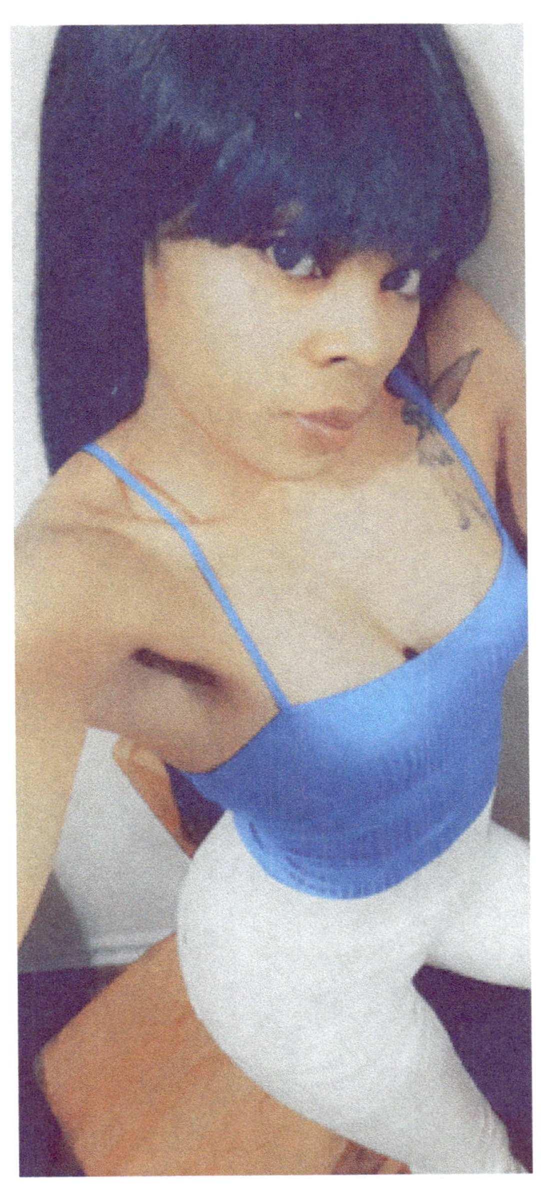

"*Shy ain't shy in the eye of fear.*"

FEMALE JESUS

She was the nature of God
Her essence was near in the willingness of man
She had to explore the richness of her gods
Wellness of her existence
Tell the world of their guidance
They life to always protect
How to carry on the words to sing in the ears of a girl

PSYCH WARD

I know everyone at my psych ward
When I'm pulling in, I gotta decide hard
No more road time
We just play cards
Sobering is fun
It brings the days far
So yeah, I know everyone in my psych ward

ONE OF A KIND

We were people in different kind
Directed to the presence in human you will find
Dark places in heaven, the labor is wild
Because the math became deeper
Then Southern was like wise
Caution was like a hat, with no burden inclines
Separation was like a class motivated to combine

BEAT

Leading with controlling
Healing but I'm holding
Seeing what to believe in
Willing to make new roads begin
Bolding to become my own woman
Folding and let the chills within
Broken but not missing pieces we win
Together, we become a whole gathering

IT TURNS OUT

Don't want you to be like me
But it turns out you're the meanest person when It comes
to me
But it turns out
You're going hard to show me
But it turns out
Push comes to shove
But it turns out
Still taking my steps to make it work
But it turns out
Going back took some time
But it turns out
You had your last chance
But it turns out
Recruiting friends, and having together time
But it turns out
Nice knowing you
Because it turns out

TRILL

Time to evaluate
Turn this money I'm trying to conjugate
To write these speeches
I don't have time for breaks
England pounds, oh wait
Canadian doing it all day
The next top dollar I'm buying
And put it in the savings
Ask for interest
And turn in it into Trillion, Ku Klux Klan

FIRST EXPERIENCE

Some battles I can do because I have experience
Same is like a task going in blind folded
Getting it done before it starts to open
Generating the goals again
The feeling hides beyond perfect
But do it in care
To know well done was always here

ON IT

I got classy on it
His suit and tie all Hottie on it
Because we slow riding our sports car on it
Hosting our own celebration on it
Keeping it as an accomplishment on it
Just made a change and put a difference on it

KEEP IT GOING

I can't come up with one poetic style to race
I got to line it up in categories, this can't relate
The test was to keep it and operate
Put it in definitions so I can concentrate
On the words, I'm trying to elaborate
The music in the formal way

NATION

Guides to start my tribe
Let it fit in as I realize the journey as the wind
Bringing new bright
I'm going to spark up the tight
Grow it in and let it all rise
Clocks are rolling in the heights
Business as it came in disguise

TRACK

Not fast in speed but intelligence
To have a place to rock with the motion
The disaster is not fared in a cross one
But practice that trat track it will be the most run
In order to promote done
Preparation too years to begin
Well infested about that gun

TAP IT UP

He tells me to drop to my knees so he can tap his gush up
I tell him take your time, this body is neat
Tap this gusch up

Don't do all crazy, this body ain't lazy
Started relays at eight this gusch great
You can tap it up all day
So when you tap up this gusch,
being confident looks good

Hey
Got you putting a ring on it

Tap it up
Because he wants to tap it up,
Oh yay

THE THING

Ruff the thing, but don't mash it up
Tuf p the thing, slap it up
Crush up the thing, but don't break it up
Talk dirty to the thing, lick it up
Massage the thing, suck it up
Firm up the thing, squeeze it up
Dash out the thing, now hide and put it up
Let's walk out the thing, relax it up
Dance on the thing, clap it up
Balance on the thing, target it up
Come lay down on the thing, wake it up

DELUXE

My ideas or deluxe
It takes a little time for things to adjust
Been processing these things,
Thinking about how to come up
Crossing these bridges with timing
Let me hurry up
Making money is my habit,
We ain't jolly if I ain't got it
Turning tables and I'm ballin'
And I feeling you can't stop falling.

HOOK

Hook it up
Jack it up
Watch how I walk through and mash it up

Hook it up
Kick it up
Watch how I walk through and back it up

Hook it up
Tack it up
Criss cross on it, wash it up

Hook it up
Tap it up
Walk on the line and set it up

RASTA

Mango, picking in the mango tree
I'm your Rasta

Guinep eating in the yacht with me
I'm your Rasta

June plum rice on the cool beach
I'm your Rasta

Frying fish in the woods is sweet
I'm your Rasta

Roasted breadfruit like 1, 2, 3
I'm your Rasta

IN TIME

Building my houses in the mountain looking at every state
Yeah, I'm getting my fountains
Saving up all my change
Design in the forest debating on my nation
Time for an upgrade
Competing with a lot of fame
So I gotta keep that same trait
Making hits like a baseball player at his game

"Making hits like a baseball player at his game."

ABOUT THE AUTHOR

Krystal Alicia Barrett currently lives in Durham, North Carolina with her two children. She is proud of her Jamaican roots and stands tall on her values. As a multi-talented writer, creator and social media influencer, Krystal advocates for writing as a tool to find peace and manage mental health. *Sky Yah Yah* is her first book.